Countries and Cultures

Ethiopia

by Allison Lassieur

Content Consultant:
Azeb Tadesse
University of California, Los Angeles
James S. Coleman African Studies Center
Reading Consultant:
Dr. Robert Miller, Professor of Special Populations
Minnesota State University, Mankato

Capstone press
Mankato, Minnesota

Capstone Press
151 Good Counsel Drive, P.O. Box 669, Mankato, MN 56002
http://www.capstone-press.com

Library of Congress Cataloging-in-Publication Data
Lassieur, Allison.
    Ethiopia / by Allison Lassieur.
    p. cm.—(Countries and cultures)
    Summary: An introduction to the geography, history, economy, culture,
and people of Ethiopia.
    Includes bibliographical references and index.
    ISBN 0-7368-2175-9 (hardcover)
    1. Ethiopia—Juvenile literature. [1. Ethiopia.] I. Title. II.Series.
DT373.L37 2004
963—dc21   2003001906

Editorial Credits
Gillia Olson, editor; Heather Kindseth, series designer; Molly Nei, book
    designer; Alta Schaffer, photo researcher; Karen Risch, product
    planning editor

Photo Credits
Cover images: people on hillside, Corbis/James A. Sugar; stained glass at Debre
Libanos monastery, TRIP/A. Gasson

Bob Reis, 41 (bills and 50-cent coin); Bruce Coleman Inc./Eitan Simanor, 21,
22; Bruce Coleman Inc./Rod Williams, 16–17; Capstone Press/Gary
Sundermeyer, 51; Corbis/Chris Rainier, 28; Corbis/Dave Bartruff, 56;
Corbis/Earl & Nazima Kowall, 48–49; Corbis/Francoise de Mulder, 30;
Corbis/Jon Hicks, 47; Cory Langley, 11, 42; Getty Images/Hulton Archive, 13,
27, 33; Martha Smith, 41 (1-, 5-, and 25-cent coins); Michele Burgess, 1 (all), 4,
8, 18; North Wind Picture Archives, 25; One Mile Up Inc., 57 (both); TRIP/J
Sweeney, 52; Victor Englebert, 34, 38, 45, 55, 63

Artistic Effects
Digital Vision, Comstock Klips, Corbis, PhotoDisc Inc.

1 2 3 4 5 6 08 07 06 05 04 03

Contents

Fast Facts about Ethiopia

Official name: Federal Democratic Republic of Ethiopia

Location: eastern Africa

Bordering countries: Sudan, Kenya, Somalia, Djibouti, Eritrea

National population: 67,673,031

Capital: Addis Ababa

Major cities and populations: Addis Ababa (2,639,000),
Diré Dawa (208,700), Nazrét (161,800), Gonder (142,100),
Desé (123,200)

Chapter 1

Explore Ethiopia

Part of the mighty Nile River flows through the northwestern highlands of Ethiopia. The Blue Nile, known in Ethiopia as Abay, starts its journey from Lake Tana. It travels almost 500 miles (800 kilometers) and joins with the White Nile to form the Nile River. The Blue Nile provides the Nile with almost 80 percent of the water that flows between its banks.

A few miles downstream of Lake Tana, the Blue Nile thunders over a series of waterfalls called Tiss Isat. Tiss Isat means "smoking water." It is named for the clouds of mist that cover the falls. Rainbows often appear from light reflecting off the mist. The water from the falls helps create thick, tropical forests that are home to many species of monkeys and birds.

◀ Mist rises from the Tiss Isat waterfalls, creating a rainbow.

Ethiopia

Sparkling lakes and rivers are only a small part of Ethiopia's landscape. Ethiopia is a land of extremes. High, rugged mountains tower over some areas. Deep, cool gorges plunge into the earth. Rolling plains are home to a wide variety of wildlife.

Ethiopia is located on the northeastern section of Africa, called the Horn of Africa. The country shares its borders with Sudan, Kenya, Somalia, Djibouti, and Eritrea. Ethiopia is landlocked. It shares no border with the ocean.

Ethiopia covers more than 435,000 square miles (1.1 million square kilometers). It is about the size of the U.S. states of Texas, Oklahoma, and New Mexico combined.

Ethiopia is a country with great ethnic diversity. It is known as the "cradle of humanity" because of the fossils of ancient human ancestors found there. Today, Ethiopia has more than 67 million people. More than 78 ethnic groups make Ethiopia a unique, multi-cultural country.

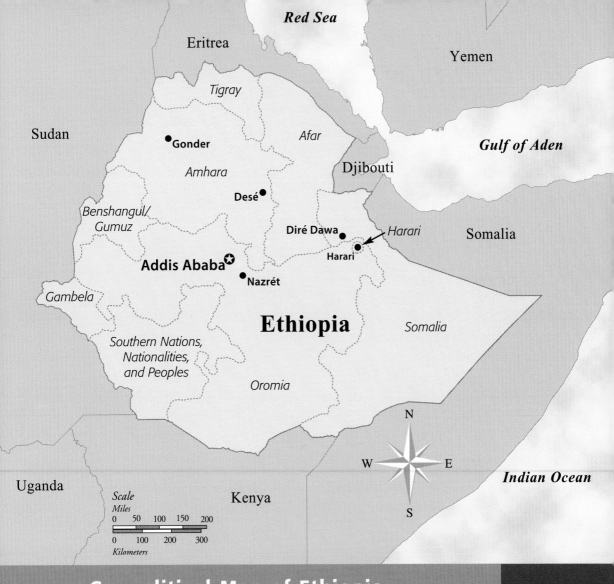

Red Sea

Eritrea

Yemen

Sudan

Gulf of Aden

Tigray

Afar

•Gonder

Djibouti

Amhara

Somalia

Desé•

Benshangul/
Gumuz

Diré Dawa

Harari

Harari

Addis Ababa ✪

Somalia

•Nazrét

Gambela

Ethiopia

Southern Nations,
Nationalities,
and Peoples

Oromia

N

W   E

Uganda

S

Scale
Miles
0   50   100 150   200

Indian Ocean

Kenya

0   100   200   300
Kilometers

Geopolitical Map of Ethiopia

KEY

✪ Capital

● City

- - - State boundaries

Fast Facts about Ethiopia's Land

Area: 435,184 square miles (1,127,127 square kilometers)

Latitude and longitude: 8 degrees north latitude, 38 degrees east longitude at Ethiopia's geographic center

Highest elevation: Ras Dashen, 15,158 feet (4,620 meters)

Lowest elevation: Denakil Depression, 410 feet (125 meters) below sea level

Ethiopia's Land, Climate, and Wildlife

Ethiopia is made up mostly of a mountainous area called the Ethiopian Plateau. This high-elevation area is split down the center by the Great Rift Valley. Nearer to the country's borders, the highlands slope down to plains.

Great Rift Valley

The main land feature in Ethiopia is the Great Rift Valley, which runs from northeast to southwest across the country. The rift marks the line where two sections of Earth's crust, called tectonic plates, are separating. This separation forms a huge valley, marked by volcanoes, depressions, gorges, lakes, and other land features. The entire Great Rift Valley stretches from Zambia in Africa to Syria in the Middle East. It runs for more than 4,500 miles (7,200 kilometers).

◄ Lake Abiata is just one of the Rift Valley lakes in southwestern Ethiopia.

In Ethiopia, the Great Rift Valley contains many lakes. The two largest Rift Valley lakes are Chamo and Abaya. Hippopotamuses and Nile crocodiles live in and near these lakes. Another valley lake, Lake Abiata, is shallow. The water reaches only 4 feet (1.2 meters) deep. Birdwatchers can view the hundreds of types of birds that live around the lake.

The Great Rift Valley gradually widens toward Ethiopia's northern border. Near Ethiopia's border with Eritrea, the rift contains an area 410 feet (125 meters) below sea level, called the Denakil Depression.

The Highlands

The Ethiopian Plateau is also called the highlands region. The highlands are more than 4,900 feet (1,500 meters) above sea level and cover about 40 percent of the country's land area. Most of the highlands contain rugged mountains with forests and lakes. The region is separated into the western highlands and the eastern highlands by the Great Rift Valley.

Ethiopia's western highlands are generally higher in elevation than the eastern highlands. Ethiopia's most famous national park, Simien Mountain National Park,

▲ Many people live in simple houses in rural parts of Ethiopia's highland region.

is in the Simien Mountains of the western highlands. Ras Dashen, Ethiopia's highest mountain, is located inside the park. Ethiopia's capital, Addis Ababa, is located in the western highlands. The highlands are crisscrossed by steep river valleys, including the Omo River and Blue Nile River valleys.

The eastern highlands area includes flat-topped mountains called ambas. The area also includes gorges, ravines, and jagged mountain peaks.

Lowlands

The highlands slope down to lowland areas. Generally, the lowlands are hotter and drier than the highlands. Poor soil makes the land difficult to farm. Few people live in the lowlands.

The main lowland areas are the southeastern Ogaden Plateau and the northern lowlands along the border with Sudan. The Ogaden Plateau makes up most of the eastern lowlands. The Dawa, Wabe Gestro, and Wabe Shebele Rivers flow across the plateau. In the north, the highlands drop off suddenly into grasslands along the border with Sudan.

▼ A woman gathers branches in Ethiopia's flat, dry Ogaden Plateau.

13

Climate

Ethiopia's temperatures range from hot to mild. The country's lowlands can get very hot. The Denakil Depression may reach 120 degrees Fahrenheit (49 degrees Celsius). In the high elevations, Ethiopia's temperatures stay mild. In the highlands, temperatures average between 60 and 70 degrees Fahrenheit (16 and 21 degrees Celsius).

Rainfall in Ethiopia depends mainly on elevation. The central highlands receive between 31 and 47 inches (79 and 119 centimeters) of rain every year. Areas in lower elevations might get 16 inches (41 centimeters) or less in a year.

Since the 1980s, lack of rainfall has severely affected Ethiopia. A series of droughts have killed crops. Drought is especially common in the eastern and northeastern areas.

Plant Life and Wildlife

Though Ethiopia still has large forested areas, these forests are being cut down quickly. Today, forests cover about 20 percent of Ethiopia. Most trees grow on the mountains and woodland plains. Farmers cut down the trees to make room for livestock.

The rest of Ethiopia consists of grasslands and dry, near-desert areas. The lowland areas, especially near

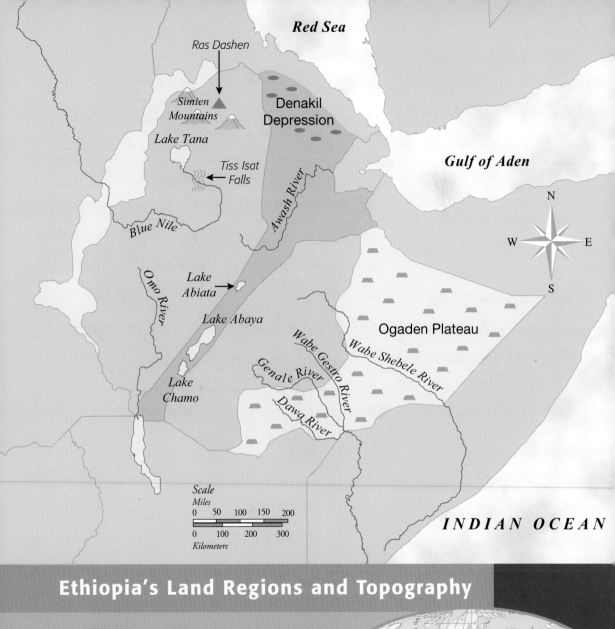

Red Sea

Ras Dashen

Simien Mountains

Denakil Depression

Lake Tana

Tiss Isat Falls

Gulf of Aden

Awash River

Blue Nile

Omo River

Lake Abiata

Lake Abaya

N

W · E

S

Ogaden Plateau

Wabe Gestro River

Wabe Shebele River

Genale River

Lake Chamo

Dawa River

Scale
Miles
0   50   100   150   200

0   100   200   300
Kilometers

INDIAN OCEAN

Ethiopia's Land Regions and Topography

KEY

☐ Lowlands

☐ Great Rift Valley

☐ Highlands

⬭ Depression

⬢ Plateau

▲ Mountain

⛰ Mountain Range

〰 River

〰〰 Waterfall

15

Gelada Baboon

The magnificent gelada baboon can be found in Ethiopia's Simien Mountains. Male gelada baboons are easily recognized by the tufts of fur around their faces. They also have a patch of hairless skin on their chests. Adults weigh between 25 and 45 pounds (11 and 20 kilograms) and stand about 2 feet (.6 meter) tall.

Gelada baboons spend their days grazing. They sit for hours, gently pulling up blades of grass. The baboons also eat fruit, insects, flowers, and leaves. They prefer to spend the night on rocky ledges.

People used to hunt gelada baboons. Today, it is against the law to hunt this protected animal.

▲ Male gelada baboons' skin patches turn from pink to red when they are angry or agitated.

Sudan, contain plains of long grasses. The dry areas of the south contain low desert bushes called scrub.

Ethiopia has 28 endemic species of animals. Endemic animals live only in a specific area. The Ethiopian wolf, also called the Simien fox, is one of the country's endemic species. It lives in lowland grasslands within the borders of Bale Mountains National Park. Only about 500 Ethiopian wolves are left in the world. A type of antelope called the mountain nyala is another species endemic to Ethiopia. The walia ibex is a type of goat found in the wild only in Simien Mountain National Park.

Ethiopia has many other large and small mammals. The gelada baboon lives in Simien Mountain National Park. Near the Omo River in southwestern Ethiopia, cheetahs, zebras, giraffes, elephants, and other typical African animals roam. Meat-eating animals often feed on Ethiopia's rodents. One rodent, the giant molerat, makes huge networks of underground tunnels. These molerats live in large communities, similar to ants.

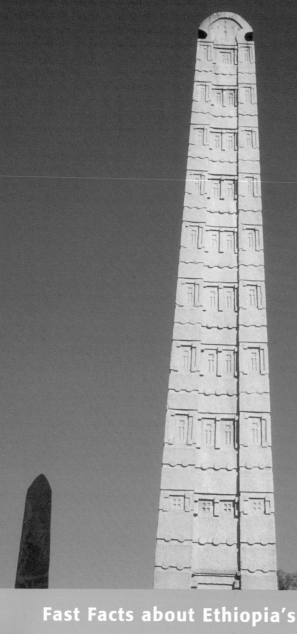

Fast Facts about Ethiopia's History

First empire founded: A.D. 200 (Aksum)
Current constitution ratified: 1994
National holiday: National Day, May 28
Current type of government: federal republic
Chief of state: president
Head of government: prime minister

Chapter 3

Ethiopia's History and Government

Ethiopia's history began long before recorded history began. Scientists believe that the first humans lived in the Great Rift Valley. Fossils of early human ancestors were found in Ethiopia. The fossils date from more than 4 million years ago. These fossils led people to call Ethiopia the "cradle of humanity."

Aksum Empire

Early Ethiopians gradually formed societies. They farmed and tended livestock. By 1000 B.C., Ethiopians were trading with people from Arabia across the Red Sea. Northern Ethiopia and present-day Eritrea became trade centers.

Gradually, an empire formed in the very northern part of present-day Ethiopia. By A.D. 200, the Aksum Empire controlled the Red Sea coast, growing rich by trading goods with Greece, Egypt, and Rome. Around

◀ People of the Aksum Empire created this tall column.

A.D. 330, Aksum's ruler, Emperor Ezana, became a Christian. Christians follow the teachings of Jesus Christ, whom they believe is the son of God. Many Ethiopians soon adopted the new religion. The Aksum Empire remained powerful until the 600s.

Beginning in the late 600s, Muslim Arabs gained power in many areas around Aksum. Muslims follow Islam. They follow the teachings of the prophet Muhammad. Their holy book is called the Qu'ran.

The Arabs cut off Aksum's trade with other empires. The Aksum Empire grew less powerful. It moved southward across the Ethiopian highlands. It spread the Christian religion and took control of different groups in that area. This southward expansion continued over hundreds of years. Meanwhile, fighting occasionally took place between Christians and Muslims in northern Ethiopia.

In 1137, the Zagwe dynasty came to power in the Ethiopian highlands. This Christian family of leaders created many churches, including the stone churches of Lalibela, which remain today.

In 1270, Yekuno Amlak took control of the highlands. He claimed to be a descendant of the Aksum rulers. The Aksum rulers claimed to be descendants of King Solomon of Israel and the Queen of Sheba, mentioned in the Bible. Amlak and his descendants

became known as the Solomonic dynasty. They ruled parts of Ethiopia until 1974.

European Contact

In a battle during the 1530s, Muslims gained control over much of the Solomonic kingdom. The Solomonic king, Lebna Dengel, wrote to the Christian Portuguese government asking for help fighting the Muslims. The

▲ Ruins at Gonder date from the 1600s. Emperor Fasiladas made Gonder his home.

Portuguese came in 1543. Although Dengel had died by that time, his son Galadewos, with Portuguese help, regained Solomonic territory.

Soon, more Portuguese came to Ethiopia. Many Ethiopians grew wary of foreign plans for the area. In the 1630s, Ethiopia sent all European foreigners out of the country. After that, few European nations maintained contact with Ethiopia.

The Empire of Gonder

Emperor Fasiladas became ruler of Ethiopia in 1632. He established his home in the city of Gonder, north of Lake Tana. Gonder became the capital of Ethiopia under Fasiladas's rule. For the next 100 years, Ethiopian art and architecture blossomed.

Still, Ethiopia did not have a strong central government. The emperor ruled over a series of subkingdoms, each with its own leader. These leaders were very powerful, and the emperor often lost control over the subkingdoms.

In the late 1700s, one leader, Ras Mikael Sehul, became especially powerful. He raised large armies and ordered the murder of two of the last Gonder emperors, Iyoas and Yohannis II. Ras Mikael Sehul's takeover signaled a new chapter in Ethiopian history. Ethiopians call this time "Zemene Mesafint," which means "Era of Princes." Leaders controlled their own regions and battled one another for more power. Although emperors still ruled Ethiopia, they had little real power.

Centralization and Foreign Interest

Beginning in the early 1800s, a series of emperors regained central power in Ethiopia. Tewodros II ruled from 1855 to 1872. Early on, he put down rebellions by regional leaders, trying to bring all of Ethiopia under one rule. Yohannis IV began his rule in 1872. He fought foreign powers and struggled to keep the empire together. One struggle was with Menelik II, who succeeded Yohannis in 1889. Menelik II regained much of the control lost during the Era of Princes. He also moved the capital to Addis Ababa.

During Tewodros', Yohannis', and Menelik's rules, Great Britain, Italy, and France became interested in Ethiopia. Italy formed settlements in present-day Eritrea in 1882. From the coast, the Italians began to move farther inland. They hoped to make Ethiopia a colony. The Italians and Ethiopians fought several

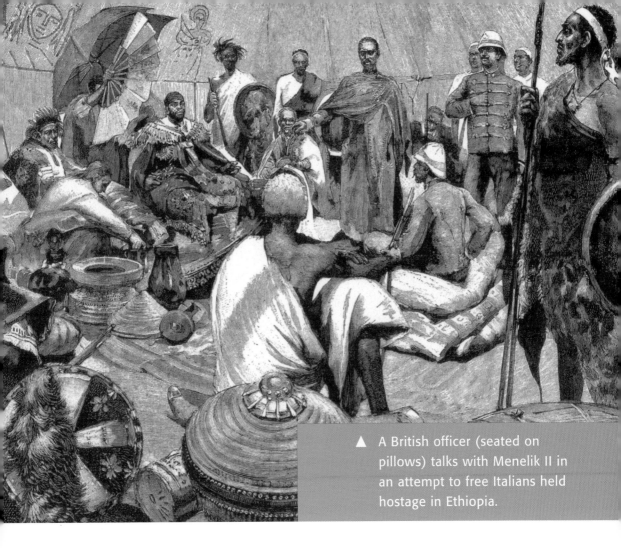

▲ A British officer (seated on pillows) talks with Menelik II in an attempt to free Italians held hostage in Ethiopia.

battles. Menelik II made a treaty with the Italians in 1889, but he withdrew the treaty when disagreements arose. Italy continued to push inland, and the two countries met in the Battle of Adwa in 1896. The Ethiopians defeated the Italians, winning respect from the rest of the world. The Italians remained on the coast.

Haile Selassie and Italian Occupation

Menelik II died in 1913. Prince Iyasu succeeded him, followed by Menelik's daughter Zawditu. In 1930, Ras Tafari became emperor and renamed himself Haile Selassie. This name means "might of the trinity." He established an education system and other modern government services.

In 1936, Italy invaded Ethiopia. It marked the only time a foreign power occupied Ethiopia. Emperor Selassie fled to England. Allied troops of Ethiopia and the United Kingdom defeated the Italians in 1941. Selassie soon returned to Ethiopia and remained in power until 1974.

The Military Takes Control

Ethiopia experienced a widespread lack of food, called a famine, in 1972 and 1973. People blamed the lack of food on Selassie's unwillingness to ask other countries for help. In 1974, a group of soldiers, called the Derg, overthrew Selassie. Lieutenant Colonel Mengistu Haile Mariam led this group. The Derg killed members of the royal family, government ministers, and other government officials. Emperor Selassie was imprisoned and soon died in jail.

The Derg established a socialist government. In socialism, a country's resources, including industries

The Italians ride through Addis Ababa during the occupation.

and land, are owned by all people. The government usually runs the industries, trying to act for the good of the people. The Derg soon enacted land reform. They seized land from former nobles and gave it to the people who actually farmed it.

Although the Derg said they wanted better opportunities for people, they ruled the people by

▲ Camels were used to deliver supplies to areas of famine during the 1980s. Camels can survive with less water than many other animals.

force. Opposition groups formed to overthrow the Derg, but government armies killed and imprisoned those who opposed the government. Thousands of people died. In 1977, Mengistu Haile Mariam officially became Ethiopia's president. He continued the government's policy of silencing all opposition.

Wars and Famine

Mengistu faced many problems during his presidency. In 1977, Somalia entered Ethiopia, hoping to claim land along the border between the two countries. People in the Eritrea and Tigray regions also began to fight against the Derg.

In the 1980s, severe droughts caused crops to fail in Ethiopia and other African countries. Without crops, people went without food. More than 5 million people depended on food from relief organizations during the famines. Warfare and other factors kept relief organizations from delivering the food where it was most needed.

A New Government

Internal conflicts increased as the Derg continued to have problems dealing with warfare and famine. In 1991, opposition groups finally overthrew Mengistu. He fled the country, and the Derg was removed from power.

The opposition groups formed the Transitional Government of Ethiopia (TGE). This government was made up of an 87-member Council of Representatives. In 1994, an elected legislature ratified a new

constitution. In 1995, Ethiopians were able to participate in elections for national government.

Government

Ethiopia is made up of nine states. The four states in northern Ethiopia are Tigray, Afar, Amhara, and

Benshangul/Gumuz. Harari, Oromia, Gambela, and Somalia lie in the south. The ninth state is Southern Nations, Nationalities, and Peoples. These states are self-governing and represent different ethnic groups in Ethiopia. Each state has executive, legislative, and judicial branches.

The national government is also made up of legislative, executive, and judicial branches. The legislative branch is made up of two houses, the House of People's Representatives and the House of Federation. Members of both houses serve five-year terms. The House of People's Representatives has 548 members elected by popular vote. The House of Federation has 108 members representing 58 ethnic groups across the country. State legislatures elect these members. The legislative branch introduces and passes new ideas for laws.

Ethiopia's executive branch includes the prime minister and president. The prime minister is elected by members of the House of People's Representatives. Both houses of the legislature elect the president, whose role as head of state is mostly ceremonial. Both the president and prime minister serve five-year terms.

Ethiopia's Supreme Court heads the judicial branch. This court makes final decisions on cases appealed from lower courts.

Ethiopia Today

Eritrea broke away from Ethiopia in 1993, but part of the border between the two countries was not clearly defined. Ethiopia and Eritrea fought a war over this border from May of 1998 to June 2000. A formal peace agreement was signed in December 2000.

Today, the country is fighting a war against the human immunodeficiency virus (HIV). HIV damages people's immune systems, making them unable to fight off diseases. The last stage of this virus is referred to as acquired immunodeficiency syndrome (AIDS). People eventually die from illnesses their bodies cannot fight. HIV has no cure. HIV has spread rapidly through many African countries. According to some estimates, Ethiopia is third in the world in its number of HIV cases.

In many ways, Ethiopia has become stronger in the last 10 years. The government is stable. People have again turned their attention to the economy. Rains have been heavy enough to sustain crops. International businesses are starting companies in Addis Ababa and other large cities.

▲ An Ethiopian soldier waits to go to the front during the border war with Eritrea.

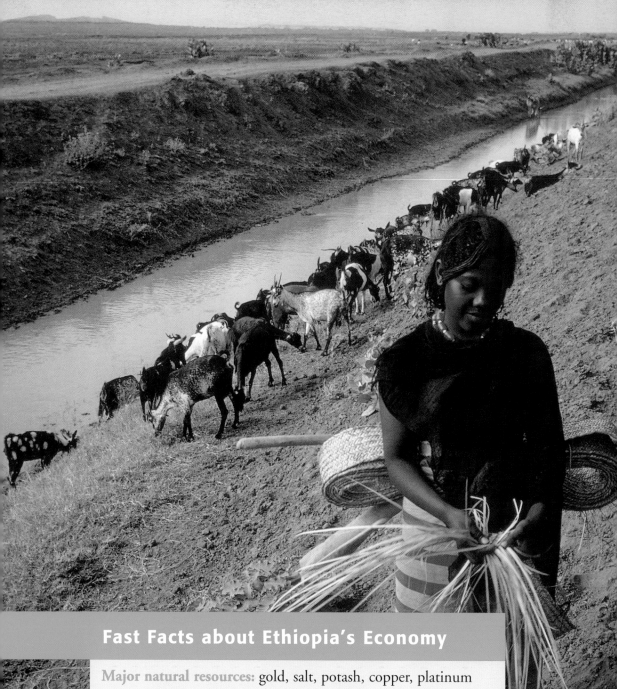

Fast Facts about Ethiopia's Economy

Major natural resources: gold, salt, potash, copper, platinum

Major agricultural products: coffee, teff, wheat, oilseeds, meat

Major manufactured products: processed food, textiles, cement

Major imports: food, chemicals, machinery, vehicles, oil

Major exports: coffee, gold, leather products, salt

Chapter 4

Ethiopia's Economy

During the years of warfare and famine, the Ethiopian economy suffered. The current government has made steps toward reform. Many state-run businesses will become privately owned. The government is developing regulations to help revive the economy. The country still has much work to do.

Agriculture

About 85 percent of Ethiopians work in farming. The country has rich soil, but the farming industry faces many problems. Droughts kill many crops. Cutting down trees for farmland and grazing land leads to soil erosion. Most farmers cannot afford modern machinery and must use simple tools and plows. Bad roads make it hard to get crops to market. Still, most Ethiopians continue to be farmers.

◀ A woman tends a herd of goats in the Great Rift Valley. She holds a palm leaf mat that she is weaving.

Coffee is Ethiopia's most valuable crop. It brings in the most money through export. About 15 million Ethiopians are involved in the coffee industry by growing, processing, trading, or transporting the crop. More than 90 percent of all Ethiopian coffee comes from small, local farms in the south.

Ethiopian farmers also grow and export pulses and oilseeds. Pulses include lentils, peas, and beans that are often sold dried. Oilseeds include soybeans, sesame seeds, sunflower seeds, and other seeds used to make oils. Niger seeds are a type of oilseed native to Ethiopia.

Ethiopians grow many crops to feed themselves and their families. Many Ethiopian farmers grow a tiny grain called teff. Teff is endemic to Ethiopia. Ethiopians use teff to make a bread called injera. Injera is a large part of people's diets all over the country. Many farmers also grow corn and sorghum. Sorghum is a grain often made into flour. Wheat is ground into flour and cut for its straw. People use the straw to feed their animals and to make roofs for their houses. In the cooler highland areas, farmers grow barley. Most of the barley is used to make local drinks.

Ethiopia is said to have the largest livestock population in Africa. Ethiopians raise cattle, sheep,

Ethiopia's Industries and Natural Resources

KEY

🫘 coffee

⬤ gold

🐄 livestock

🏭 manufacturing

🫘 oilseeds

🌱 pulses

🔺 salt

🌾 teff

🌾 wheat

▼ Men pry a salt block loose from a salt bed in the Denakil Depression.

goats, and poultry. Most livestock animals are raised in the highlands.

Livestock serve many purposes. Most Ethiopian farmers raise at least a few cattle or other livestock to provide their families with meat and milk. Some Ethiopians raise large herds of livestock. They export the meat or leather made from the animals' hides. Leather products are some of Ethiopia's biggest exports.

Mining and Energy

Mining could be a valuable Ethiopian industry, but mining companies need to overcome some problems. Miners need modern equipment to produce high yields. The lack of good transportation and roads keeps companies from bringing in equipment. Some mines have shut down because of nearby warfare. When these problems are overcome, companies can begin to mine platinum, iron, limestone, and other minerals found in Ethiopia.

Salt mining and gold mining are two of the profitable mining industries in Ethiopia. The Denakil Depression has large salt deposits. Gold mines in several areas of the country continue to produce high yields.

Ethiopia has used few of its energy resources. The country does have several hydroelectric power plants on the Awash River. The other mighty rivers throughout Ethiopia could be used to create hydroelectric power. More research is needed to explore this energy source. Ethiopia may also have large oil and natural gas reserves, but companies have not yet looked into them. The country relies on imported oil.

Manufacturing, Service, and Tourism

Ethiopia has small but growing manufacturing and service industries. Large cities have many factories. Ethiopia's major manufactured products include processed food, textiles, and leather goods. In remote villages, households manufacture most of the goods they need.

While most service jobs are found in large cities, tourism often brings money to rural areas. Until recently, Ethiopia had few tourists. Warfare in the country kept people away. Today, as Ethiopia becomes more stable, tourism is increasing. People come to view Ethiopia's unique wildlife, landscape, and historic sites.

5 cent coin

1 cent coin (back)

Ethiopia's currency is the birr. A birr is divided into 100 cents, or santeems.

Exchange rates can change daily. In early 2003, 1 U.S. dollar equaled 8.57 Ethiopian birr, and 1 Canadian dollar equaled 5.79 Ethiopian birr.

50 cent coin (front)

25 cent coin

5 birr note

50 cent coin (back)

1 birr note

1 cent coin (front)

Fast Facts about Ethiopia's People

Population distribution: 85 percent rural, 15 percent urban

Official language: Amharic, though many states have their own official languages

Life expectancy: 44 years; male—43 years; female—45 years

Literacy rate: 35 percent of Ethiopians older than age 15 can read and write

45

Harari, which is also one of the country's states. The Harari refer to themselves as Ge usu', which means "people of the city." The Dorze in southern Ethiopia are famous for their woven cloth. The Mursi, who live near the Omo River, are known for the large, round lip plates that the women wear.

Housing

Most rural houses are made out of mud with grass roofs. Some villagers use tin or other metal as roofs. Rural nomads often live in tents or stick-and-grass shelters that are easy to move from place to place.

Most urban Ethiopians live in houses. Some live in apartments or small houses. Others live in makeshift houses in slums. Ethiopians with more money might live in larger houses called villas.

Religion and Traditional Beliefs

Most Ethiopians follow either Christianity or Islam. About 25 million Ethiopians are Christians. Most follow the Ethiopian Orthodox Church. A smaller group are Roman Catholic or Protestant. About 31 million Ethiopians are Muslim. Many Muslims live near the coastal nations of Eritrea, Djibouti, and Somalia. The walled city of Harari is an important Islamic area of the country.

▲ Typical rural houses sit in a village outside the walled city of Harari.

Learn to Speak Amharic

Most Ethiopians speak their own local languages. The official language of the country is Amharic. The Amharic alphabet looks different from the English alphabet. The words below are written in the English alphabet.

hello—selam (se-LAHM)

goodbye—dehna-hunu (DE-he-na-hoo-NOO)

thank you—ammessegnalehu (AM-me-se-nah-LE-hoo)

yes—awon (AH-wuhn)

no—ay-dellem (AY DELL-ehm)

please—i-bak-kiwo (ee-BAHK-KEE-woh)

Do you speak English?— Englizenya yichelallu? (in-GLI-zeen-yah yih-CHEL-al-loo)

▲ Many children learn to read and write Amharic in school.

Traditional beliefs are followed in areas where neither Christianity nor Islam have taken hold. Most of these beliefs have been followed since ancient times. These beliefs are based on the worship of natural elements such as the Sun, the Moon, the sky, mountains, rivers, lakes, and animals. More than 8 million Ethiopians follow traditional beliefs.

A small group of people are Ethiopian Jews. Most of them migrated to Israel in the 1980s. The Ethiopian Jews who are left live in the Gonder area and in the mountainous regions of Tigray.

Education

The Ethiopian government provides a free education for all children, but children are not required to attend school. About 45 percent of Ethiopian children go to school.

Children do not attend school for a number of reasons. Most Ethiopians live in rural areas with few schools. Some children need to help their families with farming. Many schools have poor facilities. Some are overcrowded and do not have enough books for their students. Teachers who speak the local languages are hard to find.

In urban areas, the schools are better. Many urban students complete high school and go on to college. Ethiopia has several universities.

The Ethiopian government realizes that the education system needs improvement. Sixty-five percent of Ethiopians cannot read and write. New education policies provide hope that more Ethiopians will benefit from education in the future.

Clothing

Ethiopians wear a wide array of clothing. Ethiopians in urban areas dress similar to people in the United States and Europe. Others wear traditional clothing. A traditional dress is the shamma. It is a length of white cotton called a netela that is wrapped around the body. Some women wear a dress called an abesha kemis. These dresses are decorated with colorful embroidery and woven borders.

Meals

Meals are an important time of day for Ethiopian families. Formal meals begin with a hand-washing ceremony. A decorative jug or jar is brought to the table. Water is poured over each guests' hands into a basin. In some areas, the meal cannot start until the head of the household has torn a piece of injera for everyone at the table.

Make Dabo Kolo

Ethiopians eat a great deal of bread and flour products. Dabo kolo looks like flat peanuts when cooked. Please ask an adult to help you with this recipe.

What You Need

Ingredients	Equipment
2½ cups (600 mL) all-purpose flour	dry-ingredient measuring cup
½ teaspoon (2.5 mL) salt	liquid-ingredient measuring cup
2 tablespoons (30 mL) sugar	measuring spoons
½ teaspoon (2.5 mL) cayenne pepper	large mixing bowl
¼ cup (60 mL) oil	cutting board
about ⅓ cup (80 mL) water	knife
	frying pan
	wooden spoon

What You Do

1. Put 2 cups (480 mL) flour, salt, sugar, pepper, and oil into a large mixing bowl.
2. Knead them together and add water as needed to form a stiff dough. Continue kneading for a few minutes longer.
3. With a small handful of the remaining flour, lightly flour the cutting board.
4. Tear off a small handful of dough. Use your palms to roll the dough into a long strip about ½ inch (1.3 centimeters) thick.
5. Cut the strip into pieces about ½ inch (1.3 centimeters) wide.
6. Repeat steps 3, 4, and 5 for the remaining dough.
7. Put the pieces into an ungreased frying pan. Cook over medium heat about 10 minutes, or until they are light brown. Turn and stir to prevent burning.

Makes 8 to 10 servings

Religious beliefs can have an impact on food. Muslims do not eat pork and certain other foods. On Wednesdays and Fridays, many Ethiopian Orthodox Christians do not eat meat, eggs, or dairy products.

Coffee is an important drink in Ethiopia. Ethiopians often perform a coffee ceremony when guests visit. Coffee beans are roasted, crushed, and steeped to make coffee. Each guest is served at least three cups from a decorative pot. The process can take up to two hours.

Holidays and Celebrations

Ethiopia follows the Julian calendar. It has 13 months. Twelve months have 30 days, and 1 month has 5 days. In leap years, the last month has 6 days. The Ethiopian new year begins on September 11 of the calendar used by the United States and Canada.

Ethiopia holds a national celebration on September 27 called Maskal. Maskal is an ancient celebration. It marks the end of the rainy season and the beginning of Ethiopian spring. Orthodox Christians celebrate it as the Feast of the True Cross. It celebrates the finding of the cross on which Jesus was crucified. The night before, people of all ages stream through the villages

◀ A woman pours hot, steamy coffee during a coffee ceremony.

53

dressed in white and carrying daisies. The next day in Addis Ababa, large parades march through the streets. At sunset, the crowd lights a huge pyramid-shaped bonfire. In smaller villages, Maskal is celebrated with feasts and parties.

Ethiopian Orthodox Christians celebrate many holidays. Christians celebrate Christmas, called Ganna (gehn-NAH), on January 7. They spend time with family and give small gifts. Christians also celebrate Timkat, called Epiphany in other countries. It honors the day the three wise men found the infant Jesus.

Muslims celebrate several Islamic holidays. One of the most well known is Ramadan. For one month, Muslims do not eat or drink from dawn to sundown. At the end of this fasting, they have a big feast on Eid al-Fitr.

Several Ethiopian holidays are unrelated to religion. On March 2, Ethiopians remember Menelik II's defeat of the Italians at the Battle of Adwa. Ethiopians honor the nation's workers on May 1, Labor Day. National Day, on May 28, celebrates the fall of the Derg in 1991.

Ethiopia's holidays and celebrations help keep the country's traditions alive. As with any nation, Ethiopia tries to keep up with an ever-changing world while maintaining its unique heritage. Ethiopia's diverse people continue to work together to shape a bright future.

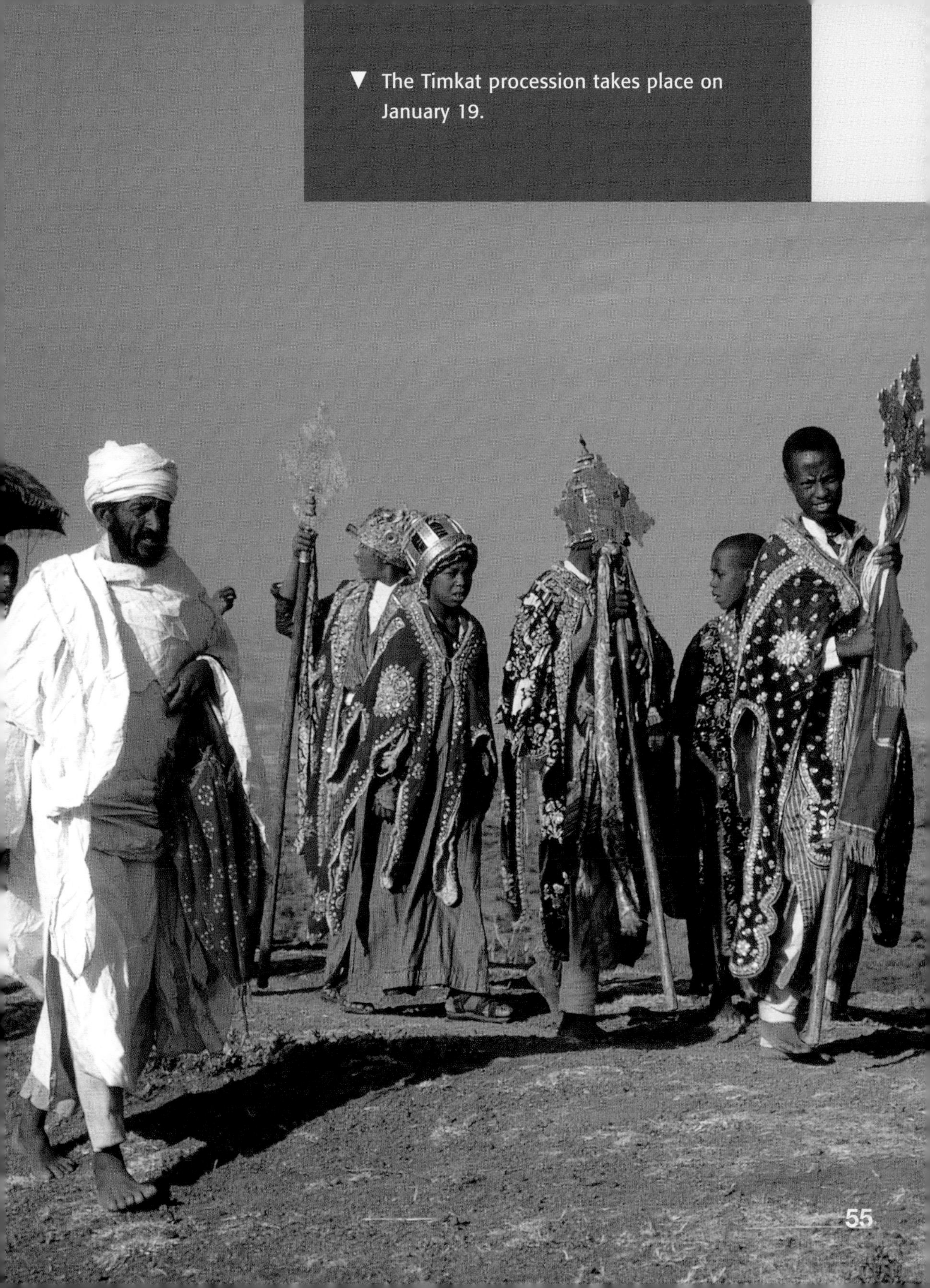

▼ The Timkat procession takes place on January 19.

▲ The Lion of Judah monument in Addis Ababa honors Haile Selassie. People often referred to him as the Lion of Judah.

Ethiopia's National Symbols

◀ Ethiopia's Flag

The Ethiopian flag has three stripes. The colors of Ethiopia's flag are known as the pan-African colors. Many other African countries adopted the same colors when they became independent. The red stripe stands for sacrifice. The green stripe represents fertility, labor, and development. Yellow stands for hope, justice, and equality. In 1996, the Ethiopian government added the National Emblem to the flag.

◀ Ethiopia's National Emblem

The yellow star on a blue disk in the middle of the flag is known as the National Emblem. The National Emblem is the symbol of the current government. It represents the desire of the Ethiopian people to live together in unity and harmony. In the past, different Ethiopian governments have put their own symbols on the flag.

National anthem: Whedefit Gesgeshi Woude Henate Ethiopia
(March Forward, Dear Mother Ethiopia)

Timeline

600s
Arab Muslims establish settlements on the Red Sea coast.

1543
Portuguese come to Ethiopia to help Ethiopian Christians defeat Muslims.

1889
Menelik II becomes emperor.

1930
Haile Selassie is crowned emperor; he establishes a modern army and an education system.

A.D.   **1100**   **1800**

A.D. 200
Aksum Empire controls the Red Sea coast.

1137
Zagwe dynasty begins.

1632
Fasiladas becomes emperor of Ethiopia and establishes Gonder as the capital.

1896
Ethiopians defeat Italians in Battle of Adwa.

1936
Italy invades and controls Ethiopia.

1994

The current Ethiopian constitution is ratified.

1941

A combined Ethiopian and U.K. force defeats the Italians; Emperor Selassie returns to power.

1977

Somalia invades Ethiopia to claim the Somali region but is defeated.

1991

Mengistu flees the country, and the Derg is removed from power.

1995

Ethiopia holds its first popular election.

1950

2000

1974

Emperor Selassie is overthrown; Mengistu Haile Mariam and the Derg come into power.

1984–1986

Ethiopia experiences a devastating famine; thousands die.

1993

Eritrea separates from Ethiopia.

2000

Ethiopia and Eritrea call a cease-fire in their border war.

Words to Know

appeal (uh-PEEL)—to ask for a decision made by a court of law to be changed

endemic (en-DEM-ik)—restricted to a specific area or location

famine (FAM-uhn)—a great lack of food that causes starvation

gorge (GORJ)—a narrow, steep-walled canyon

human immunodeficiency virus (HYOO-min i-MYOO-noh-duh-FISH-uhn-cee VYE-rus)—a disease of the immune system that makes a person unable to fight off diseases; HIV turns into AIDS; no cure exists for this disease.

injera (in-JEER-uh)—a flat, fermented bread made from teff or other grains

plateau (pla-TOH)—an area of high, flat land

pulses (PUL-suhs)—a type of crop that includes lentils, peas, and beans that are often dried

rift (RIFT)—an opening or crack

teff (TEF)—a tiny grain that Ethiopians use to make bread

To Learn More

Berg, Elizabeth. *Ethiopia.* Countries of the World. Milwaukee: Gareth Stevens, 2000.

Berg, Elizabeth. *Ethiopia.* Festivals of the World. Milwaukee: Gareth Stevens, 1999.

Corona, Laurel. *Ethiopia.* Modern Nations of the World. San Diego: Lucent Books, 2001.

Hall, John G. *Ethiopia in the Modern World.* Exploration of Africa: The Emerging Nations. Philadelphia: Chelsea House, 2003.

Laird, Elizabeth. *When the World Began: Stories Collected in Ethiopia.* Oxford Myths and Legends. New York: Oxford University Press Children's Books, 2000.

Schnapper, LaDena, ed. *Teenage Refugees from Ethiopia Speak Out.* In Their Own Voices. New York: Rosen Publishing Group, 1997.

Useful Addresses

Embassy of Ethiopia in Canada

#210-151 Slater Street

Ottawa, ON K1P 5H3

Canada

Embassy of Ethiopia in the United States

3506 International Drive NW

Washington, DC 20008

Internet Sites

Do you want to learn more about Ethiopia?

Visit the FactHound at *http://www.facthound.com*

FactHound can track down many sites
to help you. All the FactHound sites
are hand-selected by our editors.
FactHound will fetch the best, most
accurate information to answer
your questions.

IT'S EASY! IT'S FUN!
1) Go to *http://www.facthound.com*
2) Type in: 0736821759
3) Click on "FETCH IT" and FactHound will put you on the
trail of several helpful links.

You can also search by subject or book title. So, relax
and let our pal FactHound do the research for you!

▲ A nomadic woman builds a house near the Denakil Depression.

Index